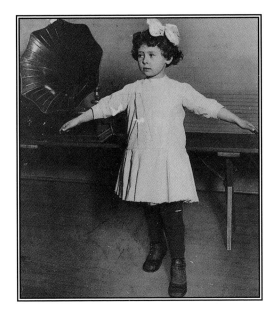

Children
of the
SETTLEMENT HOUSES

Children
of the
SETTLEMENT HOUSES

Caroline Arnold

PICTURE
the
AMERICAN
PAST

Carolrhoda Books, Inc./Minneapolis

To my mother, Kay Scheaffer, and to the memory of my father, Lester Scheaffer; to the Northeast Neighborhood House in Minneapolis, Minnesota; and with special thanks to Margaret Berry, friend and former director of the National Federation of Settlements

Front cover: Children sit on the steps of Northeast Neighborhood House, a settlement house in Minneapolis, Minnesota.
Page one: A girl listens to music at University Settlement in New York City.
Page two: Snack time at Henry Street Settlement in New York City.
Opposite page: The race begins at Telegraph Hill Neighborhood House in San Francisco.

Text copyright © 1998 by Caroline Arnold

Carolrhoda Books, Inc., c/o The Lerner Publishing Group
241 First Avenue North, Minneapolis, MN 55401 U.S.A.

Website address: www.lernerbooks.com

LIBRARY OF CONGRESS CATALOGING-IN-PUBLICATION

Arnold, Caroline.
    Children of the settlement houses / Caroline Arnold.
       p.   cm. — (Picture the American past)
    Includes bibliographical references and index.
    Summary: Explains what a settlement house is, describes its role in the lives of poor children who live near it, and tells how the settlement house movement is still being felt today.
    ISBN 1-57505-242-3
    1. Social settlements—United States—History—Juvenile literature. 2. Urban poor—Services for—United States—History—Juvenile literature. 3. Poor children—Services for—United States—History—Juvenile literature. [1. Social settlements. 2. Poor.] I. Title. II. Series.
    HV4194.A77 1998
    362.5'57'0973—dc21   97-43555

Manufactured in the United States of America
2 3 4 5 6 7 – JR – 09 08 07 06 05 04

CONTENTS

Above: Henry Street in New York City
Opposite page: In Chicago, two boys bring home bread from a bakery.

What Is a Settlement House?

Order is our basis; improvement our aim;
friendship our principle.
—boys' club motto, University Settlement, 1886

In the late 1800s, America's cities began to grow faster than ever before. People were moving to cities from farms and small towns. They also came from countries in other parts of the world. They came for jobs, freedom, and a better way of life.

New York City. Children find little room to play in a crowded tenement apartment.

Many of the newcomers were poor. They could only afford to live in rundown neighborhoods called slums. Families crowded into tiny apartments in buildings called tenements. Children played in dark stairways and dangerous alleys.

Chicago. Hull-House, a settlement house in a poor neighborhood

A few people from other parts of the city wanted to make life better in these dirty, noisy places. They moved into, or *settled*, in poor neighborhoods. They opened community centers where people could meet, take classes, get advice for their problems, and have fun. These places were called *settlement houses*. Settlement houses are also sometimes called neighborhood houses.

Chicago. Hull-House's library was free. Most settlement house activities were free or cost small amounts of money.

No matter what your age, you could find something to do at a settlement house. Babies and toddlers went to nursery care. Older children went to settlement houses for sports, crafts, clubs, parties, music lessons, and concerts. You could also check out library books or see a doctor or a dentist.

At a settlement house in New York City, you could put your money in a special savings bank for children. You could go to kindergarten and cooking classes and even take a bath!

New York City. On the rooftop of a settlement house, children enjoy the playground.

New York City. The Lower East Side became the home of the first American settlement house.

The first settlement house in the United States was started in 1886. A man named Stanton Coit rented rooms on the Lower East Side of New York City. His building was old and crowded. No one had electricity or hot water. Stanton Coit's neighbors felt sorry for him. They thought he had lost all his money and had been forced to live there. They were wrong.

New York City. The University Settlement basketball team in 1907

Stanton Coit wanted to learn how poor people lived. He became friends with his neighbors. He invited a boys' club to meet in his rooms. Soon there were more activities. This was the beginning of University Settlement.

People in other cities wanted to help the poor, too. They believed that if people of all backgrounds lived and worked together, they could make the world a better place.

San Francisco. Telegraph Hill Neighborhood House was founded in 1890.

Chicago. One of Jane Addams's first projects at Hull-House was a day care nursery for the children of working mothers.

In 1889, Jane Addams opened Hull-House, a settlement house in Chicago. The streets nearby were littered with garbage. On warm days, the neighborhood smelled awful. The flies were terrible. Jane Addams got herself appointed city garbage inspector. She made sure that all the trash was picked up around Hull-House. She worked with other people to improve the neighborhood.

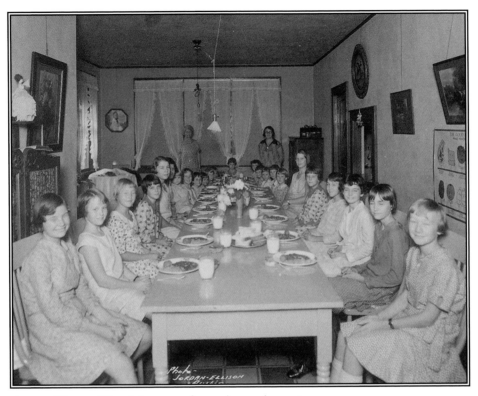

Austin, Texas. The club room of a settlement house in 1930

By 1910, there were more than 400 settlement houses in American cities. Over the next few decades, more settlement houses opened as cities grew.

Settlement houses were started by people like Jane Addams and Stanton Coit. They were started by churches, Jewish organizations, colleges, and other groups of caring people. In the city of Philadelphia, the symphony orchestra opened a settlement house where children learned to play the violin or sing.

Settlement houses were places where people learned to take pride in themselves. Phyllis Wheatley House was in a mostly black neighborhood in Minneapolis, Minnesota. In the library, children read about black heroes and black history. "We didn't get that in school," remembers one child.

Minneapolis, Minnesota. Children at Phyllis Wheatley House

Chicago. A cooking class at Hull-House, in about 1930

A typical settlement house had large meeting rooms, a gym, a library, and club rooms. Some also had a cooking room, wood shop, nursery school, coffee shop, clinic, or even a bowling alley. Most settlement houses also had apartments where some of the workers lived.

Minneapolis. Day nursery children at Pillsbury House in 1926

Daily life at a settlement house began early. In the morning, parents dropped off children for nursery school. In the afternoon, older children came for after-school clubs and sports. The sounds of laughter, music, and running feet didn't end until everyone had gone home at night after a concert, basketball game, or meeting.

Saint Paul, Minnesota. A nursery school teacher at Neighborhood House

Some settlement house workers were paid. But most were volunteers. Eleanor Roosevelt volunteered at University Settlement in New York in the early 1900s. She wanted "to do something helpful in the city where we lived," so she taught children how to dance.

New York City. Rooftop dancers at University Settlement, where Eleanor Roosevelt was a volunteer

Eleanor was amazed at the children's energy as they skipped and twirled across the floor. She knew that some of her students came after working 12 or more hours in a factory. She was glad they could have fun in her class.

Above: A woman and children from the neighborhood wear clothes from their native countries at Henry Street Settlement House in New York City. Opposite page: Children from the Hull-House neighborhood

Settlement House Neighborhoods

Hallie Q. Brown was the heartbeat of the community. From any corner of the community you could walk there.
—Dorothea Burns, who grew up
near Hallie Q. Brown House

Many people who lived in settlement house neighborhoods in the late 1800s and early 1900s were new to the United States. Most had left family and friends behind. At settlement houses, they made new friends, learned English, got advice, and took citizenship classes.

Settlement house parties, plays, and concerts brought people together from the neighborhood. They had come from many parts of the world. At settlement houses, they learned new customs and celebrated traditions of the countries they came from.

Minneapolis. Children celebrate Christmas at Northeast Neighborhood House.

Chicago. The Hull-House neighborhood

Hilda Satt was ten years old in 1892 when she moved with her family from Poland to Chicago. The Satts lived near Hull-House. "There was not a tree or a blade of grass anywhere in the neighborhood," wrote Hilda. "The only play space was the street in front of our house."

Chicago. The playground near Hull-House

Beginning in the summer of 1893, Hilda found a new place to play. She discovered swings and slides near Hull-House. Jane Addams had convinced a property owner to put playground equipment on his unused lot. This was Chicago's first public playground. Now Hilda didn't "have to dodge horses" when she played. Hilda enjoyed the playground year round. In winter, it was flooded to make an ice-skating rink.

New York City. In most tenement house apartments, water had to be heated on the stove for laundry or for baths.

When Hilda got dirty playing, it was not easy to get clean. Most apartments in the neighborhood did not have a bathroom or hot water. Hilda bathed in a washtub in the kitchen.

To help people keep clean and healthy, some settlement houses operated their own public baths. University Settlement in New York had 41 showers and 2 tubs in its basement. In summer, more than 800 people came each day to bathe!

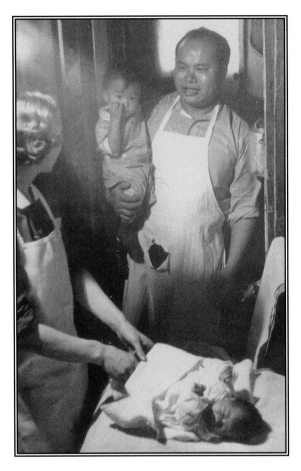

New York City. A nurse at Henry Street Settlement House gives advice.

When poor people get sick, they sometimes do not have enough money to go to the doctor. In 1893, a nurse named Lillian Wald started visiting sick people in poor neighborhoods in New York City. She helped people get well and stay healthy. Her visiting nurse service was the beginning of Henry Street Settlement House.

Telegraph Hill Neighborhood House in San Francisco was also started by nurses. If you were sick, you could go to the settlement house to see a doctor. And when you were better, you could exercise and have fun on the playground outside.

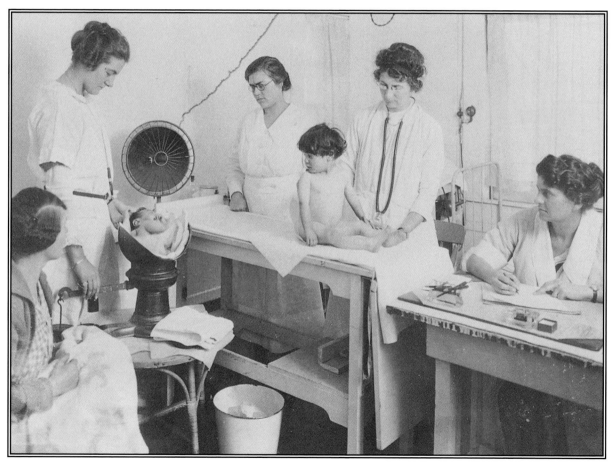

San Francisco. The clinic at Telegraph Hill Neighborhood House

Above: Boys build a clubhouse at Hull-House in Chicago.
Opposite page: Members of the Hull-House doll club meet.

A Place to Have Fun

The gymnasium was like an oasis in a desert on Halsted Street. Hundreds of boys...could go to the gymnasium and play basketball till they were so worn out that they could only go home and go to bed.
—Hilda Satt, remembering the gym
at Hull-House

In crowded city neighborhoods, children had no place to play after school. Many children joined clubs at settlement houses.

Girls often spent afternoons making crafts, cooking, or practicing puppet plays. At Hull-House, girls in the doll club shared their favorite dolls at meetings.

Many boys enjoyed building and woodworking. "Our supply of wood came from crates donated by the Montgomery Ward warehouse two blocks from the settlement," wrote a boys' club leader in Chicago in the 1930s. The boys made corner shelves and letter holders.

Chicago. In winter, children exercise in the gymnasium at Hull-House.

When ice and snow covered outdoor playgrounds, a good place to exercise was the settlement house gym. At Phyllis Wheatley House in Minneapolis, Minnesota, many boys learned how to box in the gym. One boy later said that boxing helped give him confidence and the will to succeed in life.

Minneapolis. The girls' softball team of Phyllis Wheatley House, photographed in 1925

You could play basketball, baseball, and other sports at settlement houses. Both boys' and girls' teams competed with teams from other neighborhoods.

Settlement houses were also centers for the arts. You could go to a settlement house to learn painting or pottery or to look at an art exhibit. Paintings from the Metropolitan Museum of Art in New York hung right on the walls of University Settlement.

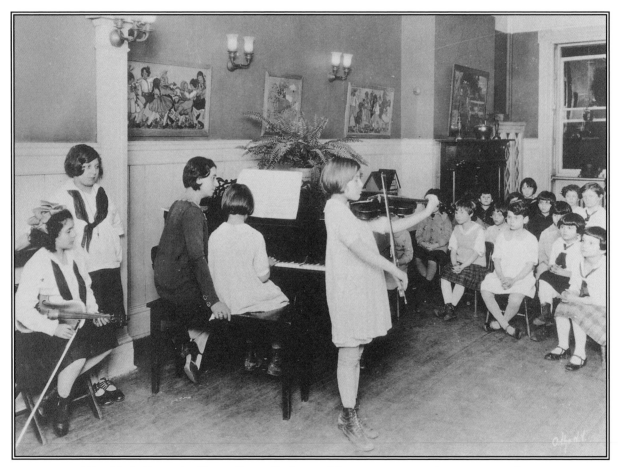

New York City. At Henry Street Settlement House, musicians play in a recital.

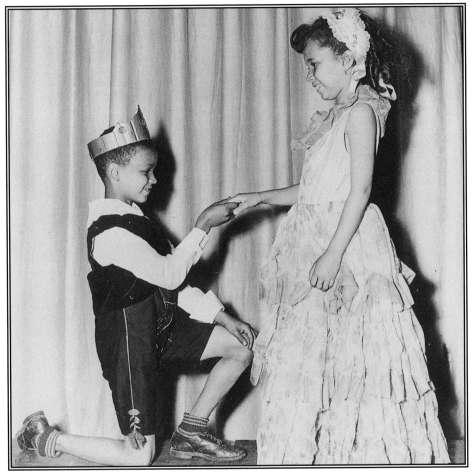

Saint Paul. A young actor and actress perform in a play at Hallie Q. Brown House in 1948.

At settlement houses, there were music and dance lessons, plays and concerts. Many actors and musicians got their start in settlement house classes.

Westchester, New York. Children go swimming at Henry Street Settlement House's summer camp.

Most children who lived near settlement houses had spent their whole lives in the city. They never saw a forest or watched the stars at night until they went to a settlement house summer camp. At camp, city children spent the day hiking, boating, swimming, fishing, making crafts, and playing games.

Beacon, New York. Gathering around the campfire at the University Settlement summer camp

At night, they sang songs and roasted marshmallows around a campfire. Then, as they fell asleep in their cabins or tents, they listened to the sounds of owls and other nighttime animals.

Between the late 1800s and the mid-1900s, many things changed. New laws improved health and safety. Cities built parks and playgrounds, libraries and public baths. Most new houses and apartments had hot running water and electricity. People working at settlement houses had helped bring about many of these changes.

Saint Paul. Children take archery lessons at Hallie Q. Brown House in about 1950. By the 1950s, many settlement houses were changing. Hallie Q. Brown changed its name to the Hallie Q. Brown Community Center.

New York City. Children work in the art room at University Settlement.

Neighborhoods also changed. New people moved in, while others moved out. Some settlement houses closed. Others changed to meet new needs in the neighborhood. Whether they are called settlement houses, community centers, neighborhood centers, or drop-in sites, they are still places where people are working to make life better for everyone in the community. And they are always places where you can go to make friends, solve problems, and have fun.

Author's Note

The settlement house movement started in 1884 in a working-class district of London, England, at a place called Toynbee Hall. The founder of Toynbee Hall, Samuel Barnett, lived in the neighborhood so he could get to know the people as a friend and neighbor. Barnett also tried to improve his neighbors' lives. He asked university students to come to Toynbee Hall to talk to the neighbors about books and ideas.

Jane Addams, Stanton Coit, and other Americans visited Toynbee Hall and were impressed by this way of helping the poor. They put these ideas into practice in the United States.

In the late 1800s and early 1900s, there were few government programs in the United States for helping the poor. People in need had to depend on the charity of private citizens and settlement houses for help with their problems. Later, during the Great Depression of the 1930s, the United States government began a variety of social welfare programs. These programs replaced many of the services once provided by settlement houses.

Since then, settlement houses have become one of many institutions serving the needs of people in American cities. Though many settlement houses have changed since the early years, the idea of working as friends and neighbors to help people solve problems remains the same.

SETTLEMENT HOUSE TREATS

A Recipe for Popcorn Balls

Holiday parties were always a high point of the year at settlement houses. They were a time when everyone from the neighborhood could enjoy being together.

Hilda Satt's first visit to Hull-House was at a Christmas party. Hilda was Jewish and had never seen a Christmas tree or heard carols before. She went to the party feeling frightened but soon felt very much at home. "Everybody seemed to be having a good time," Hilda remembered later. "No one seemed to care where they had come from, or what religion they professed, or what clothes they wore, or what they thought."

In the 1950s, when I was growing up in Minneapolis, Minnesota, I always looked forward to the children's Christmas party at the Northeast Neighborhood House. The auditorium was filled with fragrant evergreens and colorful decorations. We played games, sang songs, and watched the drama club put on a play. One year I was an actor and played the part of the littlest angel! At the end of the party, each child always received a small gift and a popcorn ball wrapped in colored paper. I still remember the sweet and crunchy taste.

Here's how you can make your own popcorn balls.

Popcorn Balls

2 cups light corn syrup

1 cup sugar

2 tablespoons white vinegar

½ cup (1 stick) butter or margarine

1 cup cold water

food coloring (optional)

3 quarts popped, unsalted, and
    unbuttered popcorn*

disposable aluminum roasting pan

waxed paper

butter or vegetable oil spray

plastic wrap

ribbon

1. In a large saucepan or electric skillet, stir together corn syrup, sugar, vinegar, and butter. Ask an adult to cook the mixture: The adult must first bring syrup mixture to a boil. Adult should lower heat to simmer, then continue stirring for 5 minutes.

*To make three quarts popcorn, start with 1 cup unpopped corn.

2. Fill a small bowl with cold water. Ask adult to drop a small spoonful of hot syrup mixture into water. As soon as syrup is cool enough to handle, try shaping it into a soft ball. If syrup forms a ball, ask adult to remove pan from heat or turn off electric skillet. (If syrup does not form a ball, ask adult to continue cooking and repeat cold-water test.) Let syrup cool for 15 to 20 minutes, or until cool enough to handle. Add food coloring if desired.

3. Place popped popcorn in disposable aluminum roasting pan. Pour syrup over popcorn. Stir gently to coat popcorn with syrup.

4. Place large spoonfuls of syrup-covered popcorn on waxed paper. Butter clean hands or spray clean hands with vegetable spray. Then take popcorn and shape into balls with hands. Wrap popcorn balls in plastic wrap and tie shut with ribbon.

Makes 16 to 20 medium size (3-inch) popcorn balls. Syrup mixture may be prepared in advance and refrigerated until needed. Before using, reheat briefly in microwave oven. For a quick microwavable alternative, start with 3 quarts popcorn. Melt ¼ cup (½ stick) butter or margarine, 6 cups miniature marshmallows, and one 3-ounce box flavored gelatin in a microwave-safe bowl. Stir to mix. Pour mixture over popcorn. Form popcorn balls as directed in steps 3 and 4 above.

Note to Teachers and Adults

For children, the early years of settlement houses may seem like part of a far-off past. But there are many ways to make this era and its people come alive. Along with helping children cook up those holiday treats, popcorn balls, you can explore America's settlement house past in other ways. One way is to read more about settlement houses, and more books on the topic are listed on page 46. Another way to explore the past is to train young readers to study historical photographs. Historical photographs hold many clues about how life was lived in earlier times.

Ask your children or students to look for the details and "read" all the information in each picture in this book. For example, how do the tenement house apartments shown on pages 8 and 27 differ from a typical modern apartment? (Most modern apartments are equipped with hot and cold running water and have full bathrooms.) Why are so many very young children shown at settlement houses? (Settlement houses often offered the only local day care, nursery care, and kindergarten classes.)

To better learn to read historical photographs, have young readers try these activities:

Reporting on Settlement Houses

From the point of view, or perspective, of one of the children shown in this book, write an article for the school newspaper describing the settlement house in your neighborhood. Study the photographs of activities at settlement houses. Then try to answer these questions in your article: Why do you go to the settlement house? What are your favorite things to do there? What sorts of things can you do at the settlement house that you can't do anywhere else?

Coming to America

Many of the people who came to settlement houses in the late 1800s and early 1900s were originally from a foreign country. They often lived in immigrant neighborhoods like the one shown on page 6. Going to a settlement house—where they could learn English, get advice, and learn new customs—helped these immigrants adjust to life in a new country.

Did you come to America from a different country? If so, how does your new home differ from the country of your birth? If you are not a new immigrant, set aside time to interview your parents, grandparents, or other older family members. Find out when members of your family came to this country and why. Ask them if they remember going to a settlement house in their neighborhood. If a family member is an immigrant, ask that person what it was like to come to this country.

Write down your findings and read your report out loud to your classmates, family, or friends. Then listen to their reports to hear how others came to America.

Being a Settlement House Volunteer

When Hilda Satt was a teenager, she worked as a volunteer tour guide at Hull-House, showing the settlement house to visitors. Dress in costume as a settlement house volunteer in the early 1900s and show a new visitor around. Explain to your visitor—and to your audience of classmates or family—what goes on at a settlement house. Why was the settlement house founded? What goes on at the settlement house each day—and night? What activities might your new visitor be interested in? Read the text—and the photos—in this book for information and for details. To give your presentation more authenticity, read some of the books listed on page 46.

RESOURCES ON SETTLEMENT HOUSES

Hakim, Joy. *An Age of Extremes*. New York: Oxford University Press, 1994. Part of a series on United States history, this book looks at the lives of people in the late 1800s and early 1900s, when the first American settlement houses were founded.

Lewis, Barbara A. *The Kid's Guide to Service Projects: Over 500 Service Ideas for Young People Who Want to Make a Difference*. Minneapolis, Minn.: Free Spirit Publishing, 1995. This book offers suggestions on ways to improve your community.

McPherson, Stephanie Sammartino. *Peace and Bread: The Story of Jane Addams*. Minneapolis, Minn.: Carolrhoda Books, Inc., 1993. McPherson follows the life story of one of the founders of the American settlement house movement, the woman who started Hull-House in Chicago in 1889.

Polacheck, Hilda Satt. Edited by Dena J. Polacheck Epstein. *I Came a Stranger: The Story of a Hull-House Girl*. Urbana, Ill.: University of Illinois Press, 1989. This book for adults is written by Hilda Satt Polacheck, who as a girl moved from Poland to Chicago and who regularly went to Hull-House.

Saller, Carol. Illustrated by Ken Green. *Florence Kelley*. Minneapolis, Minn.: Carolrhoda Books, Inc., 1997. Saller tells the story of Florence Kelley, who was both a volunteer at Hull-House and a tireless opponent of child labor in the early 1900s.

Website   http://www.wnet.org/tenement/
This Website links you to the Lower East Side Tenement Museum in New York City, where you can tour the rooms of a tenement house in the early 1900s.

New Words

Great Depression: the longest and severest economic slump in American history, which took place from 1929 to about 1940. During the worst days of the Great Depression, nearly half of all factory workers had lost their jobs.

settlement houses: community centers where people can meet, take classes, get advice for their problems, and have fun

slums: crowded city neighborhoods where housing and other living conditions are extremely poor

social welfare programs: programs, often run by the government, that help people obtain food, clothes, housing, or health care

tenements: buildings that are divided into many apartments. Tenements are often overcrowded, dirty, or in bad repair.

Index

TIME LINE

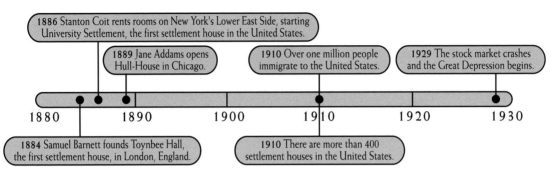

1886 Stanton Coit rents rooms on New York's Lower East Side, starting University Settlement, the first settlement house in the United States.

1889 Jane Addams opens Hull-House in Chicago.

1910 Over one million people immigrate to the United States.

1929 The stock market crashes and the Great Depression begins.

1880　1890　1900　1910　1920　1930

1884 Samuel Barnett founds Toynbee Hall, the first settlement house, in London, England.

1910 There are more than 400 settlement houses in the United States.

ABOUT THE AUTHOR

Caroline Arnold is the author of more than 100 books for young readers. Her well-received titles include *Cats: In from the Wild, Saving the Peregrine Falcon*, and *Watching Desert Wildlife*, published by Carolrhoda Books, and *Bobcats*, a Lerner Early Bird Nature Book. Ms. Arnold is a graduate of Grinnell College and the University of Iowa. She lives in Los Angeles, California.

Ms. Arnold grew up at the Northeast Neighborhood House in Minneapolis, Minnesota. Her father was the director of the settlement house, and her mother supervised the nursery school and other programs. As a girl, Caroline participated in after-school clubs and art and gym classes at the settlement house, and in summer she went to the settlement house camp in northern Wisconsin.

ACKNOWLEDGMENTS

The photographs in this book are reproduced through the courtesy of: Minnesota Historical Society, cover, pp. 17, 19, 20, 24, 33, 35, 38; University of Illinois at Chicago, The University Library, Jane Addams Memorial Collection, Wallace Kirkland Papers, back cover, pp. 10, 18, 30, 31, 32; University Settlement Archives, pp. 1, 11, 13, 21, 37, 39; Henry Street Settlement, pp. 2, 6, 22, 34 (photo by A. Tennyon Beals), 36 (photo by Paul Parker Photo); Telegraph Hill Neighborhood Center, San Francisco, CA., pp. 5, 14, 29; Collection of Catherine Scheaffer, p. 7; Brown Brothers, p. 8; University of Illinois at Chicago, The University Library, Jane Addams Memorial Collection, pp. 9, 15, 23, 25, 26; Archive Photos, p. 12; Austin History Center, Austin Public Library, #C03250, p. 16; Corbis-Bettmann, p. 27; Provided by Henry Street Settlement, courtesy of Visiting Nurse Service of New York, p. 28; Laura Westlund, p. 41; Arthur Arnold, p. 48. Excerpts from *I Came a Stranger: The Story of a Hull-House Girl* by Hilda Satt Polacheck, edited by Dena J. Polacheck Epstein (Urbana: University of Illinois Press, 1989), appear on pages 25, 26, 31, 41 and on the back cover of this book.